Copyright © 2008 Simple Truths, LLC

Published by Simple Truths, LLC
1952 McDowell Road, Suite 205
Naperville, IL 60563-6506

Design: Rich Nickel
Edited: Stephanie Trannel

ISBN 978-1-60810-002-6

Printed and bound in China

simple truths®
THE GIFT OF INSPIRATION

www.simpletruths.com
(800) 900-3427

01-4CPS-08

Nature's Inspiration

A Photographic Journey

by Ken Jenkins and Peggy Anderson

The joy of the unknown welcomes us each morning as we peer at the world outside. A sparrow chooses our windowsill to usher in a new day with the most delightful of songs. Trees appear and disappear in the passing fog, and mist moves and soothes our heart. Simplicity becomes wonder as we experience life and weather in its purest form.

The wonder stirred within us by nature is a combination of amazement and admiration that is inspiring. Inspiration so real and unassuming that we spontaneously find deeper meaning in the scenes, sounds and smells we encounter. Nature's inspiration is as simple as deer browsing in a meadow, or the peaceful rhythms of a rolling stream. We continually build on these experiences. They encourage and excite us…and are often required to sustain and motivate us as we travel along our journey.

The inspiring encounters in my life have been abundant beyond what I could ask or think. Surely it's not only that my occupation involves extended periods of time in the wilderness. Each day I wake with a desire to be touched by things that are good and real and pure. Whether on a congested highway as I travel to an appointment or during that time I have reserved for quiet, nature awaits with a new presentation of wonders both large and small.

Regardless of how full and involved our days have become, we have the opportunity to be stirred by that which man has neither made nor improved upon. That which we are invited to participate in with the joy of a child and the heart of a saint. The poet W.H. Davies so beautifully wrote, "What is this life if, full of care, we have no time to stand and stare? No time to stand beneath the boughs and stare as long as sheep or cows."

Nature's response is often in direct proportion to our approach. When I am expectant and walk peacefully, the birds sing sweeter and the smells seem richer. On many occasions I have encountered wildlife that react more from curiosity than from alarm. A ruffed grouse has flown from his perch to welcome my intrusion into his elusive world. Deer, elk and mountain goats have indirectly approached until they "nose" my nearby pack or bed for a nap. Quite often on a high country ridge a raven flies in to keep me company.

These experiences are common to all who patiently wait for nature to inject something gentle and heartening into our days. To have "eyes to see and ears to hear" is at first a discipline and eventually a habit…a constantly rewarding lifestyle. The investment required is usually no more than a glance, and the return is a smile and warmth that enriches and stimulates our lives.

Walk with me while I introduce you to some of the thousands of subjects that continue to amaze me. The invitation is echoed in every wisp of wind and every roll of thunder. Every note of song from our feathered friends says, "look and listen to the natural world and receive her good tidings."

Ken Jenkins

Caribou Browsing in Shadow of Mt. McKinley
Denali National Park, Alaska

My face stung in the crisp air of a September morning as I waited for sunrise. The blanket of frost that coated the blueberry bushes crunched with each step until I gave in, remaining motionless...silent, absorbing all that lay before me. Caribou browsed on sweet reindeer mosses, a favorite food. They had noted my approach but quickly returned to peaceful grazing. Wonder Lake, sculpted by massive glaciers many years ago, lay in the mid-ground. The lake, and the river that feeds it, is a healthy habitat for loon to raise their young, moose to feed on aquatic vegetation, and Cutthroat and Dolly Varden to spawn and thrive. Towering in the background is magnificent Mt. McKinley, 20,310 feet in elevation. The sunlight has lit the eastern flanks of the great mountain and the frost has lifted from the ridge beyond the lake. In a few contemplative moments I'm able to absorb an assortment of life lessons. The massive Alaska Range gives all else perspective. As I coexist with wildlife I am reminded of the essential need to practice restraint and respect nature. The quiet and the light and the calm become indescribable and deeply affect my soul.

NATURE IS THE ART OF GOD.
~Dante Alighieri

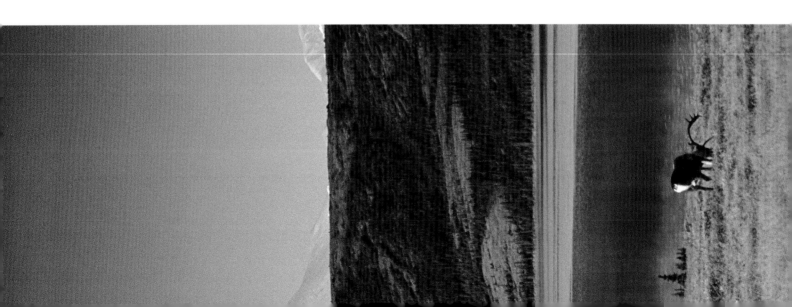

MORNING MIST IN GIANT SEQUOIA GROVE
Sequoia National Park, California

8

TREES ARE OUR BEST ANTIQUES.

~Alexander Smith

AN ANIMAL'S EYE HAS THE POWER
TO SPARK A GREAT LANGUAGE.

~ *Martin Buber*

BOBCAT POISED IN PINE
Montana

My photographic career began in the Great Smoky Mountains of East Tennessee with a couple of books on the black bear. That was well over 30 years ago, yet my fascination with the black bear goes back much further. From the time I could walk, we camped and hiked in those ol' Smokies alongside the black bear; I learned to respect and enjoy every sighting. This black bear cub, however, is from the Northwoods of Minnesota. I watched a sow and her two cubs as they inspected the morning woodlands. After a few trips up and down a hardy birch, one youngster discovered a well-suited boulder for a nap. The curvature of the stone was an ideal "cradle" for this growing bruin. Everything in his young life will have purpose and meaning as he becomes stronger and rests and listens and learns.

ALWAYS KEEP ONE STILL, SECRET SPOT
WHERE DREAMS MAY GO.

~ Louise Priscoll

13

FORGET NOT THAT THE EARTH DELIGHTS TO FEEL YOUR BARE FEET
AND THE WINDS LONG TO PLAY WITH YOUR HAIR.

~ *Kahil Gibran*

POST STORM SUNRISE
Great Smoky Mountains, Tennessee

TURN YOUR FACE TO THE SUN AND
THE SHADOWS FALL BEHIND YOU.

~ Maori Proverb

17

**PROFILE OF GREY WOLF
IN AUTUMN BLUEBERRY FOLIAGE**
Northern Minnesota

THE STRENGTH OF THE PACK IS THE
WOLF, AND THE STRENGTH OF THE
WOLF IS THE PACK.

~ Rudyard Kipling

GREY WOLVES AT RIVER CROSSING
Kettle River, Minnesota

PATIENCE, PERSISTENCE AND TIMING REAP REWARDS.

~ Margaret Woods

GRIZZLY CATCHING SILVER SALMON

Brooks River, Alaska

In the mid-seventies, I began traveling to the southwestern parts of Alaska to photograph the coastal grizzly, or Brown Bear as it is referred to in the North. The falls along the Brooks River were becoming popular as a gathering place for bears because salmon pooled there as they made their leap upstream during migration periods. In early July, the river is running full and swift. The bears position themselves on top of the falls in a current that would sweep away the strongest human, but a large bear can weigh 1500 pounds and stand nine feet tall. The mouth is fixed and the stand is made. Salmon jump to the right, to the left, and eventually right up the center. Seldom does the bear lose his catch, allowing him to gain up to 300 pounds in the summer. Everything in his pursuit is dependent upon a single factor: timing, as are the important pursuits in all of our lives.

MORNING BREAKS IN FOREST
Northern California

LANGUAGE . . .

HAS CREATED THE WORD "LONELINESS"

TO EXPRESS THE PAIN OF BEING ALONE.

AND IT HAS CREATED THE WORD "SOLITUDE"

TO EXPRESS THE GLORY OF BEING ALONE.

~Paul Johannes Tillich

CASCADES ALONG ROARING FORK
Tennessee

THE PEBBLE IN THE BROOK
SECRETLY THINKS ITSELF A PRECIOUS STONE.

~Japanese Proverb

It is easy to take a morning walk for granted when you grow up in a rural area filled with wonder and beauty. It was wonder and beauty I was about to encounter early one day when a female deer pranced right up to me and then scampered away, as if to invite a chase. Having experienced this behavior many times in late spring, I knew it could only mean that her newborn fawn was nearby. Her seeming playfulness was an attempt to distract intruders from its whereabouts. After a brief survey of the surrounding terrain I saw the delicate beauty peering from a bed of flowering trillium. It is instinctual for the newborn fawn to find a quiet and concealed place in which to be still and gain the necessary strength for the days ahead. We, too, can gain strength in quiet stillness.

MAY THE STARS CARRY YOUR SADNESS AWAY.

MAY THE FLOWERS FILL YOUR HEART WITH BEAUTY,

AND MAY HOPE FOREVER WIPE AWAY YOUR TEARS.

~ *Chief Dan George*

FLOWERING PHLOX AND PHACELIA
ON FOREST FLOOR
Great Smoky Mountains, Tennessee

SOME THINGS HAVE TO BE BELIEVED TO BE SEEN.

~ *Ralph Hodgson*

MOUNTAIN LION
TRANSPORTING CUBS
IN HIGH COUNTRY
Bitterroot Mountains, Idaho

In our country's remote wilderness, many touching moments are exhibited far from human observation. I was privileged to watch a powerful female mountain lion moving her cubs to a new den. She carefully picked up each cub by the neck and transported it along rugged terrain to a safe and remote location. One at a time the tiny cubs went limp, seeming to sleep, as each completely trusted its mother to choose the right place for the next phase of its life. Trust is a powerful element. Accomplishment and success directly depend on what we trust and how fully we submit to that trust.

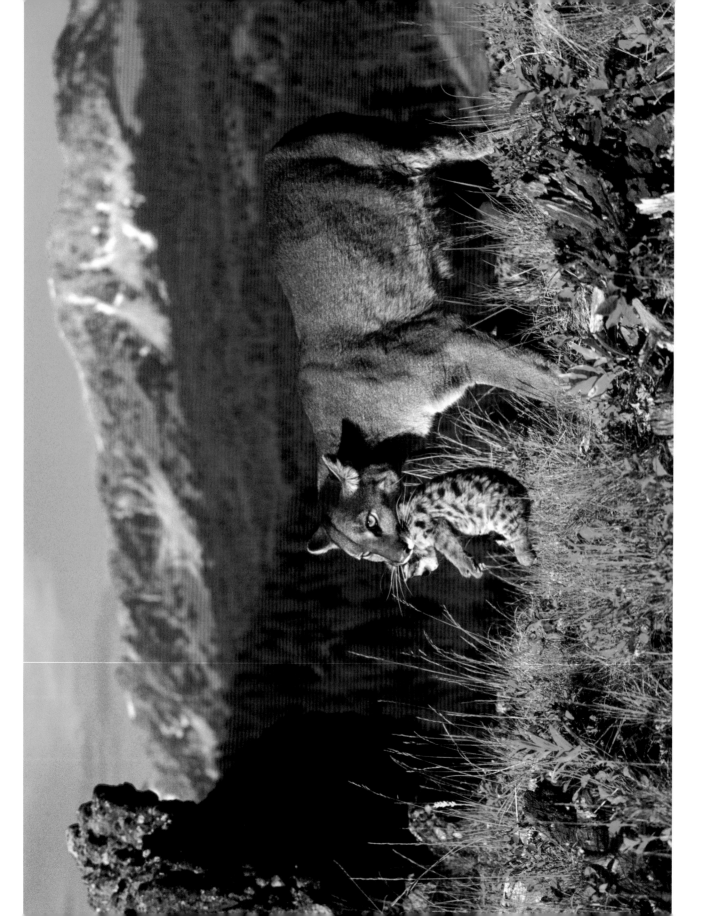

SPRUCE FLATS FALLS
Great Smoky Mountains, Tennessee

IN EVERY WALK WITH NATURE
ONE RECEIVES FAR MORE
THAN HE SEEKS.

~John Muir

Most walks in nature have an intended purpose. Sometimes it's exercise, sometimes it's to soak up a little peace and quiet, and sometimes it's to reach a particular destination. On this day, I walked for more than an hour, sensing air fragrant with summer blooms and the earthy smells of the forest. In the distance I heard the muffled sound of falling water, and as I stepped out of the dense woodlands, the sight of a steady cascade greeted me. The mist cooled and refreshed the air. I couldn't resist the urge to soak my feet in the chilly waters. As I sat and meditated on things greater than myself, I became relaxed, restored and reminded that life's diversions are steppingstones upon which our journey becomes clearer.

GREY WOLF CROSSES
SNOWY MEADOW
Southern Ontario, Canada

TO DISCOVER THE MAGIC AND WONDER OF NATURE
IS TO BE IN TUNE WITH THE RHYTHM OF THE EARTH.

~ Peggy Anderson

MORAINE LAKE
Canadian Rockies

I DO NOT COUNT THE HOURS I SPEND IN
WANDERING BY THE SEA.

~ Ralph Waldo Emerson

37

TO A MIND THAT IS STILL, THE WHOLE UNIVERSE SURRENDERS.

~ *Chang Tsu*

REFLECTIONS OF AUTUMN COLORS
Upper Peninsula, Michigan

39

**BALD EAGLE SOARS
OVER SNOWY PEAKS**
Alaska

So much has been written about the eagle that we often struggle for a fitting adjective to describe her. For more than twenty years, I've observed the bald eagle's behavioral patterns in her remote habitat across North America. This morning, I climbed a high ridge above the Bering Sea in Alaska. Heavy cloud cover loomed over the partially snow-covered landscape. Only yards in front of me, the mountain had been sheared away by years of contact with wind and water. A rugged nest, possibly weighing as much as a ton, sat on the ledge below. As the morning sun stole under a cloud, an eagle pair passed by the cliff calling to their young. Gawky eaglets perked up knowing that food was not far behind this awakening. In this isolated, inclement location, plagued by storms and predators, it occurred to me that there is always strength in encouragement. The young are encouraged by familiar sounds of comfort and love. The mature are encouraged by their young's response to their outpourings.

WHEN THOU SEEST AN EAGLE,
THOU SEEST A PORTION OF GENIUS;
LIFT UP THY HEAD.

~William Blake

EAGLE AND YOUNG ON NEST
Aleutian Islands, Alaska

THE CLEAREST WAY INTO THE UNIVERSE
IS THROUGH A FOREST WILDERNESS.

~John Muir

LUSH FOREST FLOOR
Greenbrier River, Tennessee

SUNRISE ON ALASKA RANGE
Denali National Park, Alaska

44

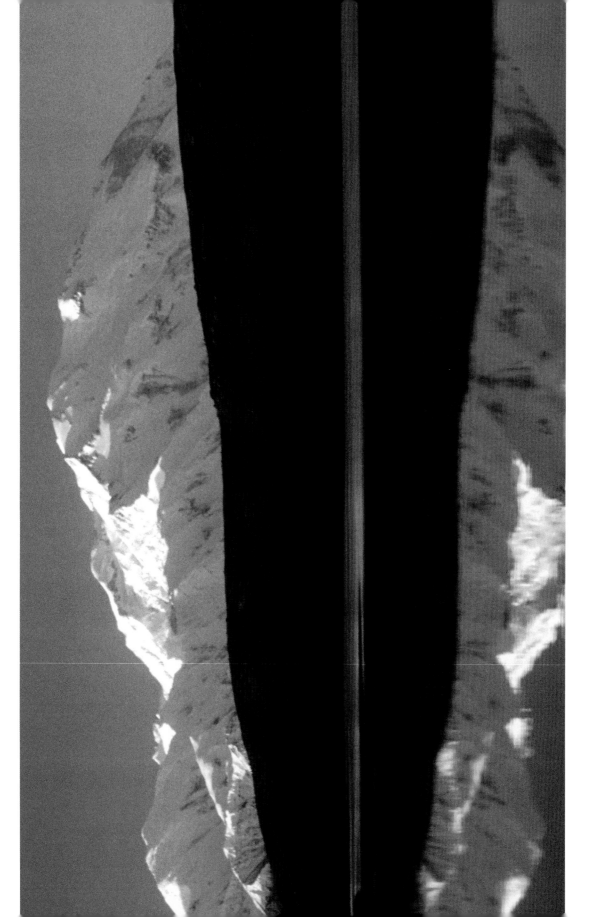

THE DAY, WATER, SUN, MOON, NIGHT —
I DO NOT HAVE TO PURCHASE THESE THINGS WITH MONEY.

~Plautus

BEHOLD THE MAJESTIC BEAUTY OF THE WILD.

~ M.C. Leban

MOUNTAIN LION RESTS
Sandstone Canyon, Arizona

**MORNING MISTS ABOVE
THE BOW RIVER**
Alberta, Canada

LISTEN TO THE BEAT OF THE OCEAN

LISTEN TO THE SONG OF THE FOREST

LISTEN TO THE PRIDE OF THE MOUNTAIN

LISTEN TO THE WHISPER OF THE MEADOW

LISTEN TO THE RHYTHM OF THE EARTH

LISTEN TO THE PASSION OF YOUR HEART

LISTEN TO THE DESIRE OF YOUR SOUL

LISTEN TO THE LESSONS OF YOUR JOURNEY

LISTEN TO THE UNITY OF CREATION.

~ Peggy Anderson

GRIZZLY
Naknek Lake, Alaska

50

GRIZZLY CUB ON SNOW
Alberta, Canada

BLACK BEAR CUB NAPPING IN TREE FORK
Bob Marshall Wilderness, Colorado

Most of us have special places we return to because they reward our souls. In the seventies and early eighties, the Katmai region of southwestern Alaska was one of my very special places. The people were few and the bears were plenty, drawn by an exceedingly abundant supply of fish. I came along the lake shore one evening to enjoy the sun's reflective pastels on the snow-covered peaks in the distance. A lumbering "crunch" signaled the approach of an old bear headed for a late meal of salmon at the river. He knew I was there, and I knew where he was headed. I didn't move or make a sound and he did not tarry nor look my way. Mutual respect allowed both of us to remain undisturbed on what proved to be a very peaceful evening.

LOSS IS NOTHING ELSE BUT CHANGE, AND
CHANGE IS NATURE'S DELIGHT.

~ Marcus Aelius Aurelius

STORM-BREAK OVER
THE SOUTH RIM
Grand Canyon, Arizona

SHAFTS OF LIGHT
PENETRATE MORNING MISTS
Sequoia National Park, California

IF I WERE TO NAME THE THREE

MOST PRECIOUS RESOURCES OF LIFE,

I SHOULD SAY BOOK, FRIENDS, AND NATURE;

AND THE GREATEST OF THESE,

AT LEAST THE MOST CONSTANT AND ALWAYS

AT HAND IS NATURE.

NATURE WE HAVE ALWAYS WITH US,

AN INEXHAUSTIBLE STOREHOUSE OF THAT WHICH

MOVES THE HEART, APPEALS TO THE MIND,

AND FIRES THE IMAGINATION;

HEALTH TO THE BODY, A STIMULUS TO THE

INTELLECT, AND JOY TO THE SOUL.

~John Burroughs

TWIN WHITE-TAILED FAWNS

Tennessee

THE WISDOM OF NATURE SPEAKS TO US HEART TO HEART,
AND NATURE'S FIRST LANGUAGE IS BEAUTY.

~Tim McNally

RED FOX PAIR ON FROZEN RIVER BAR

New Wood River, Wisconsin

57

Oak in Meadow Opens Arms to a Rising Sun

Cades Cove Meadow, Great Smoky Mountains, Tennessee

Many a morning begins with a shroud of fog or a passing shower, and I have learned to enjoy these mornings for their subtle beauty. A heavy mist only revealed giant silhouettes as I ventured further into the valley. In the foreground loomed a large white oak, her massive branches resembling arms reaching out to the morning sun. Light and mist are all that the old oak has ever required to grow grand amounts of shade in summer and habitat for both bird and mammal throughout the year. To study a tree is quite informative, and to think of all that a tree endures is most heartening. Joyce Kilmer was exactly right in his poem about the tree: "…only God can make a tree."

IF YOU WOULD KNOW STRENGTH AND PATIENCE,
WELCOME THE COMPANY OF TREES.

~ Hal Borland

STORM BREWS ABOVE BADLANDS
North Dakota

WE ALL LIVE UNDER THE SAME SKY,
BUT WE DON'T HAVE THE SAME HORIZON.

~ Konrad Adenauer

**BALD EAGLE IN LUPINE
AND BUTTERCUPS**
Alaska

EARTH TEACH ME QUIET –
AS THE GRASSES ARE STILL WITH NEW LIGHT.
EARTH TEACH ME HUMILITY –
AS BLOSSOMS ARE HUMBLE WITH BEGINNING.

EARTH TEACH ME CARING –
AS MOTHERS NURTURE THEIR YOUNG.
EARTH TEACH ME COURAGE –
AS THE TREE THAT STANDS ALONE.

EARTH TEACH ME LIMITATION –
AS THE ANT THAT CRAWLS ON THE GROUND.
EARTH TEACH ME FREEDOM –
AS THE EAGLE THAT SOARS IN THE SKY.

EARTH TEACH ME ACCEPTANCE –
AS THE LEAVES THAT DIE EACH FALL.
EARTH TEACH ME RENEWAL –
AS THE SEED THAT RISES IN THE SPRING.

EARTH TEACH ME TO FORGET MYSELF –
AS MELTED SNOW FORGETS ITS LIFE.
EARTH TEACH ME TO REMEMBER KINDNESS –
AS DRY FIELDS WEEP WITH RAIN.

~Unknown

PREDAWN MOUNTAIN OCEAN

Tennessee

TO ME EVERY HOUR OF
THE LIGHT AND DARK IS A MIRACLE.
EVERY CUBIC INCH OF SPACE IS A MIRACLE.

~Walt Whitman

MIGHTY GROVE
OF GIANT SEQUOIAS
California

I THANK YOU GOD FOR THIS MOST AMAZING DAY,

FOR THE LEAPING GREENLY SPIRITS OF TREES,

AND FOR THE BLUE DREAM OF SKY

AND FOR EVERYTHING WHICH IS NATURAL,

WHICH IS INFINITE, WHICH IS YES.

~ e. e. cummings

POLAR BEAR STUDIES BREATHING HOLE OF SEAL

Hudson Bay, Manitoba, Canada

When observing the behavior of most mammals, it soon becomes obvious that waiting is an essential part of their lives. There is a time for everything…a time to feed, a time to rest, a time to wait, and a time to move swiftly. A polar bear at the breathing hole of a ringed seal is perhaps the greatest example of patience in the animal world. The bear is near starving and the seal has appeared only briefly over a period of hours. It's wasteful to expend a great amount of energy until the time is right to catch the seal. Therefore the polar bear waits and watches and listens and smells. Such discipline is a remarkable example for humans as we grapple with the exercise of waiting.

ADOPT THE PACE OF NATURE:
HER SECRET IS PATIENCE.

~ Ralph Waldo Emerson

CLIMB THE MOUNTAIN

AND GET THEIR GOOD TIDINGS.

NATURE'S PEACE WILL FLOW INTO YOU

AS SUNSHINE FLOWS INTO TREES.

THE WINDS WILL BLOW THEIR OWN FRESHNESS INTO YOU,

THE STORMS THEIR ENERGY,

WHILE CARES WILL DROP OFF

LIKE AUTUMN LEAVES.

~John Muir

EVENING REFLECTIONS
on WONDER LAKE
Denali National Park, Alaska

COLOR IS JOY. ONE DOES NOT THINK OF JOY. ONE IS CARRIED BY IT.

~ *Ernest Haas*

ANTELOPE CANYON SLOT
Near Page, Arizona

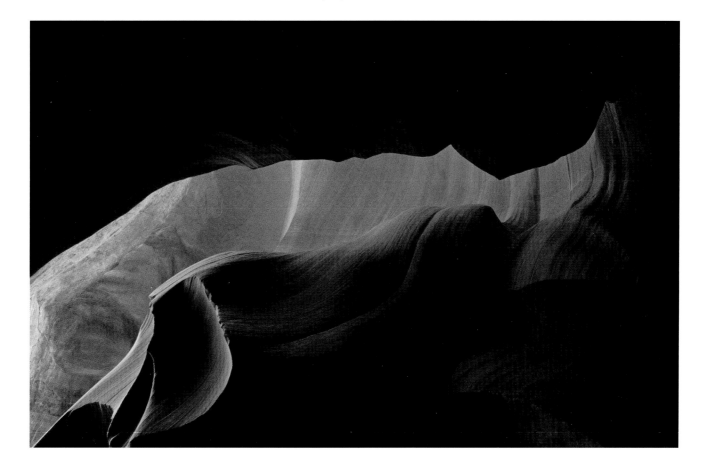

UPPER PENINSULA WATERFALL
Michigan

LIVE EACH SEASON AS IT PASSES; BREATHE THE AIR,
DRINK THE DRINK, TASTE THE FRUIT, AND RESIGN YOURSELF
TO THE INFLUENCES OF EACH.

~ Henry David Thoreau

ONE TODAY IS WORTH TWO TOMORROWS.

~ Benjamin Franklin

SUNSET AND REFLECTIONS

Swabacher Landing, Grand Tetons, Wyoming

Many years ago I learned that the most beautiful time of evening is not the literal setting of the sun, but the colorful post sunset that transforms the landscape. Swabacher Landing in the Grand Teton National Park has been the setting of movies like Jeremiah Johnson and several other western adventures. It is a quiet place to walk on an autumn evening. An hour earlier, a moose splashed in the backwaters of the Snake River and Canadian geese honked as they flew southward. Now the sun has set and there is this incredible golden-russet cast that has converted a beautiful landscape into a surreal environment of otherworldly colors. It is so quiet and so unusual that it brings silence and solace to an already soothing atmosphere.

PATIENCE AND PERSEVERANCE HAVE A MAGICAL EFFECT
BEFORE WHICH DIFFICULTIES DISAPPEAR AND OBSTACLES VANISH.

~John Quincy Adams

RED FOX IN PURSUIT OF MOUSE
Denali National Park, Alaska

My early walk through alders and blueberry bushes had been gratifying as an assortment of birds cheerfully called from the tips of dwarf birches. A moose munched on willow branches and made his way to the kettle pond nearby. I was taking a break to experience the quiet stillness of the Alaskan tundra when out of the corner of my eye I saw a red fox on morning patrol. I focused my camera as he moved through the low vegetation. Just as I thought the young fox was going to break through an opening so that I could get a clear view of him, he went "airborne!" His spring was so sudden and unexpected that I inadvertently released the shutter, capturing the entire sequence. He thought there was a potential meal living in the bushes and seized the opportunity to take what he needed in order to survive. By reaching new heights he was effective and rewarded.

AUTUMN...THE YEAR'S LAST LOVELIEST SMILE.

~ John H. Bryant

MOUNTAINS ARE EARTH'S
UNDECAYING MONUMENTS.

~ *Nathaniel Hawthorne*

ALPENGLOW ON WESTERN FACE
Mt. Rainier, Washington

83

RED FOX KIT SLEEPS ON MOTHER'S NOSE
Great Smoky Mtns., Tennessee

84

THE MOST FEROCIOUS ANIMALS ARE DISARMED
BY CARESSES TO THEIR YOUNG.

~ Victor Hugo

WILDERNESS LAKE
Mt. Robson, British Columbia

IT IS A WHOLESOME AND NECESSARY THING
FOR US TO TURN AGAIN TO THE EARTH
AND IN THE CONTEMPLATION OF HER BEAUTIES
TO KNOW OF WONDER AND HUMILITY.

~ Rachel Carson

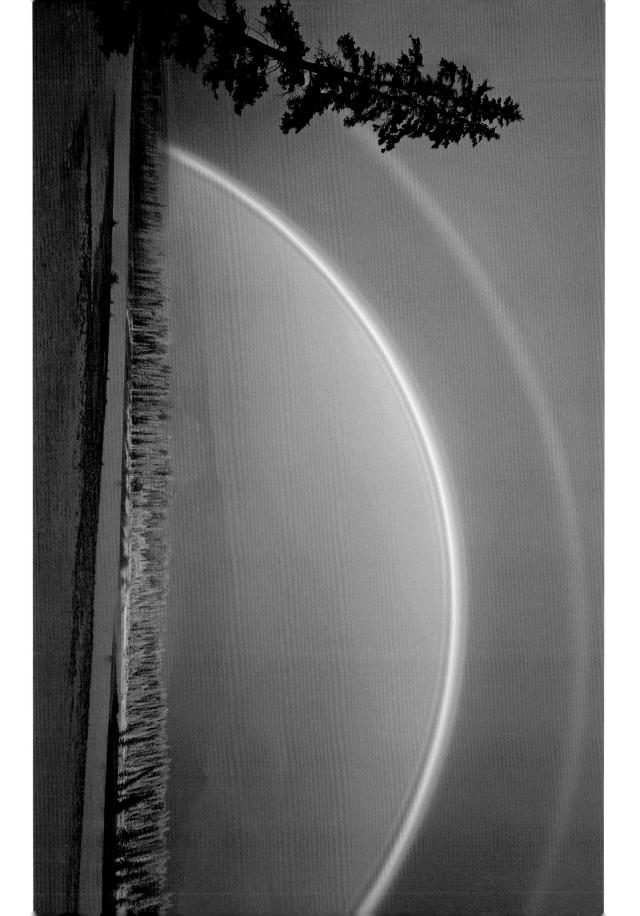

IT WAS THE RAINBOW GAVE THEE BIRTH, AND LEFT THEE ALL HER LOVELY HUES.

~*W. H. Davies*

Double Rainbow
Athabasca River, Alberta

Late June afternoons often bring welcome showers to the Canadian Rockies. Harlequin ducks gathered in the shoals of the Athabasca River as the sky became heavy. Despite a steady rain, the sun persistently filtered in along the foothills. Suddenly the western sky opened and a lemon light bathed the river at precisely the right angle. Not one but two rainbows arced across the horizon framing the sunlit forest. The spectacle reinforced what I have come to believe: no matter what the weather, there is a pleasant surprise just around the bend. I've experienced that same truth during my walk through life.

CADES COVE IN AUTUMN

Great Smoky Mountains, Tennessee

AUTUMN IS A SECOND SPRING
WHERE EVERY LEAF IS A FLOWER!

~Albert Camus

IN RIVERS, THE WATER THAT YOU TOUCH
IS THE LAST OF WHAT HAS PASSED
AND THE FIRST OF THAT WHICH COMES;
SO WITH PRESENT TIME.

~ Leonardo da Vinci

**Woodchuck Near Den
with Indian Paintbrush Blooms**

Central Minnesota

ENJOY THE LITTLE THINGS,
FOR ONE DAY YOU MAY LOOK BACK
AND REALIZE THEY WERE THE BIG.

~ Robert Brault

NEVER LOSE AN OPPORTUNITY
OF SEEING ANYTHING THAT IS BEAUTIFUL.
WELCOME IT IN EVERY FACE,
IN EVERY SKY,
IN EVERY FLOWER.

~ Ralph Waldo Emerson

COLORS THROUGH THE STORM
Canadian Rockies

Eastern Bluebirds

Rural Tennessee

The sweet songs of bluebirds are a familiar memory for those of us who spent our youth in rural areas. But when wooden fence posts began to disappear, and habitat shrank, the bluebird population declined. Today, fortunately, the popularity of birding has led to increased housing and the bluebird is back. I watched this pair search for food at daybreak. The male fed the female on a number of occasions, and at times allowed her to take the first food they discovered. It's a stirring example of shared affection and dependence that warms our hearts when we liken it to the blessings of our own relationships. Life is frequently illustrated in the simple things that surround us…if we only take time to look.

HOPE IS THE THING WITH FEATHERS
THAT PERCHES IN THE SOUL, AND SINGS THE TUNE
WITHOUT WORDS, AND NEVER STOPS AT ALL.

~ Emily Dickinson

BLACK BEAR WARMING IN MORNING SUN

Great Smoky Mountains, Tennessee

I STUCK MY HEAD OUT OF THE WINDOW THIS MORNING
AND SPRING KISSED ME BANG IN THE FACE.

~ *Langston Hughes*

SPRINGTIME BLOOMS ON DESERT

Ajo Canyon, Arizona

NATURE DOES NOT HURRY,
YET EVERYTHING IS ACCOMPLISHED.

~ Lao Tzu

MOTHER PORCUPINE NOSES HER YOUNG

Upper Peninsula, Michigan

PERSON TO PERSON, MOMENT TO MOMENT,
AS WE LOVE WE CHANGE THE WORLD.

~ *Sanahria Kaufman*

BOBCAT KITTEN
CURIOUS FROM A KNOTHOLE
Central Minnesota

105

I BELIEVE A LEAF OF GRASS IS NO LESS THAN
THE JOURNEY OF THE STARS.

~Walt Whitman

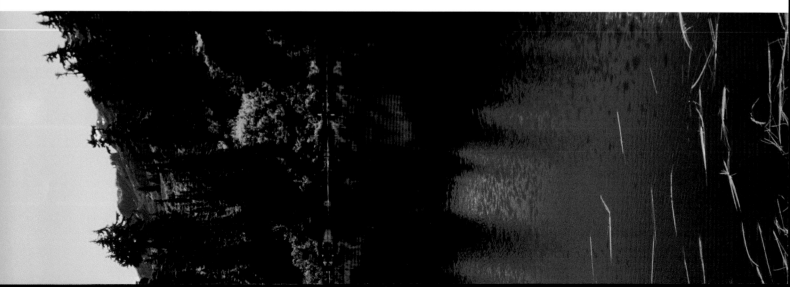

HIGH COUNTRY LAKE
North Cascades National Park, Washington

IF YOU ARE NOT WILLING TO SEE MORE THAN IS VISIBLE
YOU WON'T SEE ANYTHING.

~ Ruth Bernhard

ERMINE IN WINTER COAT
Gallatin Mountains, Montana

Along a pile of fallen logs an ermine played, darting from one opening
to the next. He is known as a short-tailed weasel during the summer
season when his coat is rich brown with a white-coated belly. In winter,
his coat becomes entirely white, and he is referred to as the ermine.
Trappers that live in the wilderness shared that an ermine is nearly
impossible to keep in captivity once he has made the transformation to
a pure white pelage. It is thought that if an ermine cannot maintain an
unsoiled coat he would rather die…and often does. The intensity of
the ermine's desire to remain clean is comparable to the human desire
to live a morally clean life.

IN THE WILDERNESS IS THE PRESERVATION OF THE WORLD.

~ Henry David Thoreau

CANADIAN LYNX
Boreal Forest, Southern Ontario, Canada

DO NOT GO WHERE THE PATH MAY LEAD.
GO INSTEAD WHERE THERE IS NO PATH
AND LEAVE A TRAIL.

~ Ralph Waldo Emerson

TINTED SUNLIGHT AFTER RAIN ON RURAL ROAD

Greenbrier, Tennessee

Young Badger Cubs on Rocky Ledge

Bridger Mountains, Montana

NOBODY, BUT NOBODY CAN MAKE IT OUT HERE ALONE.

~ Maya Angelou

LIFE IS NOT ABOUT THE BREATH YOU TAKE.
IT IS ABOUT THE MOMENTS THAT
TAKE YOUR BREATH AWAY.

~Unknown

DECEMBER DUSTING OF SNOW
South Rim, Grand Canyon, Arizona

WINTER WREN ON LICHEN-COVERED BOULDER

Pribilof Islands, Alaska

For many years I've been passionate about the works of 18th and 19th century writers whose insight and wisdom has been very beneficial to me. With very few exceptions, these writers were very appreciative of birds, and used them often in their illustrations and observations. I, too, appreciate birds; nothing in the natural world is more fascinating to me. I find that I can share their joys and behavior whether I am in Central park or on an isolated island in the Bering Sea. I watched this Winter Wren one morning as I was photographing along a cliff in the Pribilof Islands off the western coast of Alaska. Birds reinforce that age-old truth that "singing" is essential to our peace in life even when— especially when—it is the most difficult act to perform.

**BEAVER CROSSES DAM
WITH WILLOW BRANCHES**
Denali National Park, Alaska

NATURE DOES NOTHING USELESSLY.
~ Aristotle

119

**GREAT GREY OWL
IN BIRCH TREE**
Duluth, Minnesota

WISDOM BEGINS IN WONDER.

~ *Socrates*

THE SUN DOES NOT SHINE FOR A FEW TREES AND FLOWERS,
BUT FOR THE WIDE WORLD'S JOY.

~ Henry Ward Beecher

LeConte Range
Great Smoky Mountains, Tennessee

123

TO SEE A WORLD IN A GRAIN OF SAND
AND HEAVEN IN A WILD FLOWER
HOLD INFINITY IN THE PALM OF YOUR HAND
AND ETERNITY IN AN HOUR.

~William Blake

ONE TOUCH OF NATURE
MAKES THE WHOLE WORLD KIN.

~William Shakespeare (1564-1616)

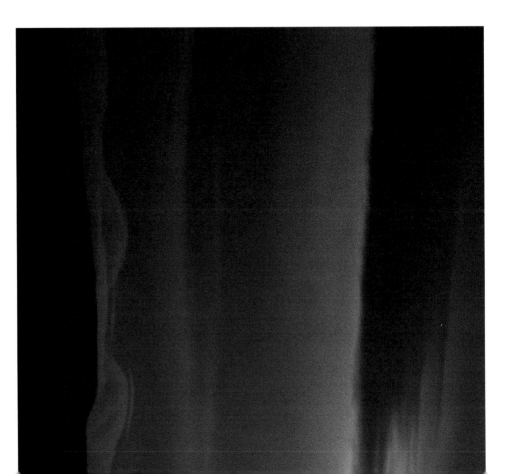

SANDHILL CRANES AT SUNSET
Bosque Del Apache, New Mexico

Whether our lives require travel or allow us to stay close to our dwelling place, we are constantly, even subconsciously, arranging our lives around the idea of "home." A motel or hotel room requires a good light, a good bed, and likely, a proper desk from which to work. It needs to provide temporary solace until we can turn our path to our own place…one that we know is equipped for our comfort and contentment. Every creature in Nature thinks in a similar way. As I waited for the sunrise, the clouds turned to many shades of pink and gold and blue. Waves of migrating Sandhill Cranes passed overhead on their long journey home, having likely endured many a fierce storm as they flew from the Canadian plains to the Desert Southwest. Hundreds of miles of trial, inconvenience, and setback had hardly frustrated their effort. The marsh-like river valley is home and their high-pitched cackles reflected great joy in having arrived.

127

Snow-covered Mountain Stream

North Carolina

IF WE HAD NO WINTER,

THE SPRING WOULD NOT BE SO PLEASANT;

IF WE DID NOT SOMETIMES TASTE OF ADVERSITY,

PROSPERITY WOULD NOT BE SO WELCOME.

~Anne Dudley Bradstreet

MAY YOU ALWAYS FIND NEW ROADS TO TRAVEL;
NEW HORIZONS TO EXPLORE;
NEW DREAMS TO CALL YOUR OWN.

~ *Unknown*

RED FOX PAUSES ON SNOWY RIDGE
Upper Peninsula, Michigan

HAY BALES
Southern Alberta, Canada

GIVE ME THE SPLENDID SUN WITH ALL ITS BEAMS FULL–DAZZLING.

~Walt Whitman

For the most part, everything in our being seems to struggle with the idea of stillness. We have become programmed to complete project after project, task after task. The thought of being idle feels inherently wrong…contrary to all that we desire to achieve. Yet it is only in the quiet, still, seemingly lonely moments that we can reflect and feel grateful. It is in those moments that we gain perspective and gather wisdom for the days ahead. In the stillness of those moments there should be no guilt, for it is rewarding to place milestones along our journey.

It was nearly midnight as I made my way back to the community of Unalaska in the very heart of the Aleutian chain of islands. I had been climbing ridges since early morning, watching eagles soar and feed their young. With my mission complete, I paused along this placid, peaceful lake and sat for a while; absorbing all that was going on before me and in my own heart. My older mountain friends call it "sorting things out." A process where a tear and a smile seem to make good company.

SUMMER BAY LAKE
Unalaska, Aleutian Islands

WE WILL BE KNOWN FOREVER BY THE TRACKS WE LEAVE.

~American Indian Proverb

LONELY POLAR BEAR
Hudson Bay Iceflow, Canada

Raft of Sea Otters
Off Baranof Island, Alaska

ALL THINGS ARE PARTS OF ONE SINGLE SYSTEM, WHICH IS CALLED NATURE;
THE INDIVIDUAL LIFE IS GOOD WHEN IT IS IN HARMONY WITH NATURE.

~ *Zeno of Citium*

139

REFLECTION POOL

Paria Wilderness, Arizona

BARBER POLE FORMATION
Paria Wilderness, Arizona

ALL OF NATURE IS A CANVAS PAINTED
BY THE HAND OF GOD.

~ Unknown

GREY WOLF SURVEYS TERRAIN FROM FROSTY CLIFF

Kettle River, Minnesota

Discovering fresh wolf tracks is one of the most exciting things that can happen in the wilderness. The tracks this morning were large and well-placed, as if their maker was on a mission. As I came to a clearing along the frozen lake I saw the wolf. He was aware of my presence long before I spotted him. From a prominent outcropping above, he stands beneath frosted pines and surveys his territory. He knows my exact location but it is of little consequence to him. Confident in his keen senses and physical abilities, he is in harmony with his territory. I watch him with a great deal of respect and am envious of his peacefulness and contentment.

WILDERNESS IS NOT A LUXURY
BUT A NECESSITY OF THE HUMAN SPIRIT.

~ Edward Abbey

WITHIN YOU THERE IS STILLNESS AND SANCTUARY TO WHICH YOU CAN RETREAT AT ANY TIME AND BE YOURSELF.

~ Hermann Hesse

CABINS IN THE AUTUMN

Alaskan Tundra

COLORADO RIVER
FLOWS THROUGH CANYON
Near Moab, Utah

146

A HUGE RED DROP OF SUN LINGERED ON THE HORIZON
AND THEN DRIPPED OVER AND WAS GONE.

~John Steinbeck

BOBCAT WITH TWO KITTENS
Eau Claire River, Wisconsin

LET THE BEAUTY OF THE WILD LEAVE FOOTPRINTS ON YOUR HEART.

~ Peggy Anderson

For the many years I have spent time in wild places, few are the hours when I have had the privilege to watch the feline species of North America. A female bobcat is very attentive and committed to her young. The kittens constantly play and explore their new world throughout the day. At regular intervals, the mother interrupts the merriment for their very favorite part of the day…a time of loving and nourishment. A sweet hum accompanies the feeding as the kittens gently suckle her milk. The mother begins to lick and groom her fragile youngsters immediately following their meal. Reassured of her constant provision and watchful eye, they drift off in an afternoon nap. The bobcat is very illusive and secretive in all her maneuverings. When kittens are born, however, the female places her life in a vulnerable position in order to give the best care and protection to her offspring.

WONDER...MUSIC HEARD IN THE HEART, IS VOICELESS.

~ Rosemary Dobson

BEARBERRY AND REINDEER MOSS ON TUNDRA
Brooks Range, Alaska

151

IN EVERY WINTER'S HEART
THERE IS A QUIVERING SPRING AND
BEHIND THE VEIL OF EACH NIGHT
THERE IS A SMILING DAWN.

~ Kahil Gibran

WINTER SCENE

Near Mammoth in Yellowstone National Park

154

**BLACK BEAR CUB
TESTS SAPLING**
*Great Smoky Mountains,
Tennessee*

THE TRUE MEANING OF LIFE
IS TO PLANT TREES UNDER WHOSE SHADE
YOU DO NOT EXPECT TO SIT.

~ Nelson Henderson

A mother bear and her three cubs crossed an enormous fallen pine that now nourishes saplings growing in its rich decay. Wonderment filled the cubs as they began smelling, tasting, and challenging their new playground. Discovering the perfect tree on top of the fallen trunk, the smallest of the three cubs reared on his strong legs pulling the sapling toward him as if to say, "you are just my size." After much testing of the little sapling's strength, the bear cub was content to sit and sniff and taste its needles. Black bears are the wisest animals that I've observed throughout my lifetime. They rarely overlook anything new in the forest and they seem to perceive changes in their habitat as opportunities to investigate and learn. The young cub's explorations make the little bear stronger, improve his agility and balance, and teach him vital information that he will need to survive in a challenging world.

LIFE IS AN ECHO; WHAT YOU SEND OUT COMES BACK.

~ *Chinese Proverb*

CATAWBA RHODODENDRON BLOOMS
Along Blue Ridge, North Carolina

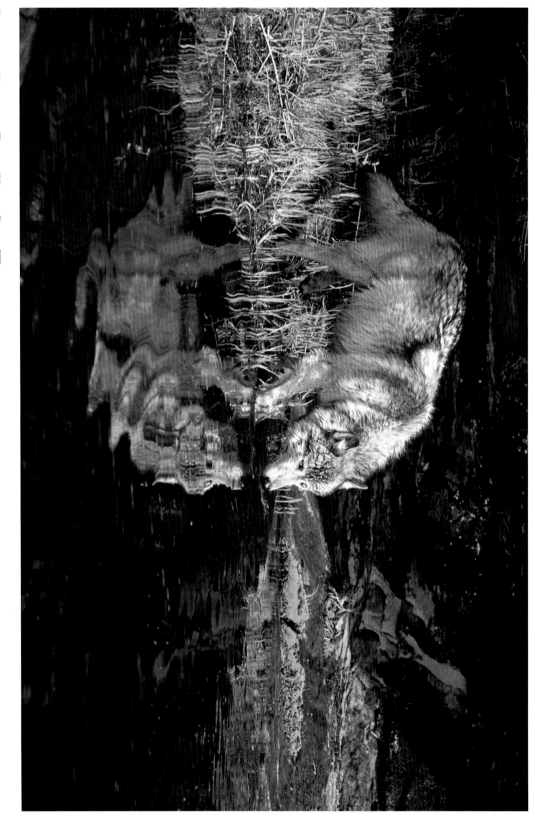

PEACEFUL EVENING RIVER VISIT, GREY WOLF

Northern Minnesota

158

THE HEART OF THE WISE MAN LIES QUIET LIKE LIMPID WATER.

~ Cameroonian Proverb

WILD MUSTANG SILHOUETTE

Pryor Mountain, Wild Horse Range, Wyoming

ONE SECRET OF LEADERSHIP IS THAT
THE MIND OF A LEADER NEVER TURNS OFF.
LEADERS EVEN WHEN THEY ARE SIGHTSEERS OR SPECTATORS,
ARE ACTIVE; NOT PASSIVE OBSERVERS.

~ James Humes

Near the Bighorn Canyon of Wyoming and in the rugged slopes of the Pryor Mountains, a remnant of America's past still live. A strong herd thrive in very harsh and rugged conditions. The wild mustangs of the Pryors roam free and have been present here for more than 200 years. The herd comes crashing down a ridge and across the meadow just in front of me. It is dusk and the lead stallion moves to a ridge where he is silhouetted against the western sky. In him is the drive to survive with the confidence and responsibility to lead his followers on the quest to be their very best against all odds.

MY SOUL CAN FIND NO STAIRCASE TO HEAVEN
UNLESS IT BE THROUGH EARTH'S LOVELINESS.

~ *Michelangelo*

MORNING LIGHT
Bow Lake, Canadian Rockies

KEN JENKINS

A native of the Great Smoky Mountains, Ken has photographed the natural world since early childhood pursuing it full time for the past 30 years. Traveling extensively throughout North America, he has led natural history treks from the Arctic to the Galapagos Islands. Ken's work has been published for years in publications ranging from *National Geographic* to *Cousteau* magazines. His books include *Great Smoky Mountains National Park*, a coffee table book, *Reflections of Wolves*, *Reflections of the Black Bear, Reflections of Grizzlies*, and a series of children's books titled *Wilderness World of...Bears,...of River Otters...of White-tailed Deer, and...of Raccoons*. His most recent book, *Expert Lifemanship*, a partnership with Dr. Warren Wiersbe features his 20 years of work with eagles as an illustration of life from a biblical perspective. Ken's galleries in the Smokies, Beneath the Smoke and Heaven's Eyes exhibit several hundred of his photographs. He splits his time between project-oriented field work, speaking engagements in a variety of settings, and writing for upcoming publications. His home is in Gatlinburg, Tennessee with his wife and partner of 30 years, Vicki.

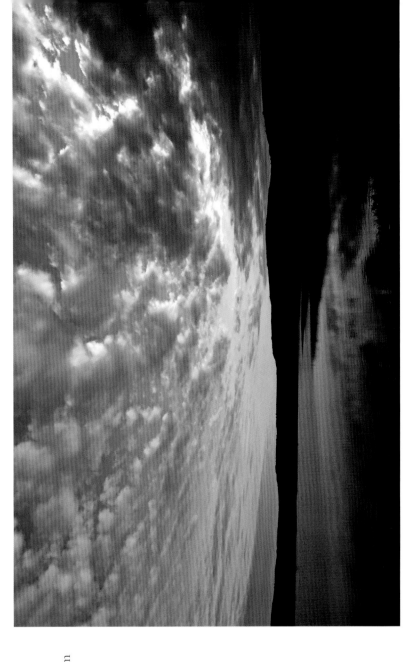

Ken's website is www.kenjenkins.com
and he may be contacted at
ken@kenjenkins.com.

Ken Jenkins
446 East Parkway, Ste. #12
Gatlinburg, TN 37738

165

THE GIFT OF INSPIRATION

THE SIMPLE TRUTHS DIFFERENCE

If you have enjoyed this book we invite you to check out our entire collection of gift books, with free inspirational movies, at **www.simpletruths.com.**

You'll discover it's a great way to inspire *friends* and *family;* or to thank your best *customers* and *employees.*

Also, our products are **not available in bookstores… only direct.** Therefore, when you purchase a gift from Simple Truths you're giving them something they can't get elsewhere!

For more information, please visit us at:
www.simpletruths.com

Or call us toll free…
800-900-3427

simple truths®
THE GIFT OF INSPIRATION